Territories of the United States

U.S. VIRGIN ISLANDS

Julia McDonnell

PowerKiDS press

Published in 2025 by The Rosen Publishing Group, Inc.
2544 Clinton Street, Buffalo, NY 14224

First Edition

Editor: Therese Shea
Book Design: Rachel Rising

Photo Credits: Cover, Terri Butler Photography/Shutterstock.com; Cover, pp. 1, 3–32 boromvit tatasai/Shutterstock.com; Cover, pp. 1, 3–32 P-fotography/Shutterstock.com; Cover, pp. 1, 7, 9, 11, 13, 19, 21, 27, 29 https://commons.wikimedia.org/wiki/File:Flag_of_the_United_States_Virgin_Islands.svg; p. 4 zmotions/Shutterstock.com; pp. 5, 15 Rainer Lesniewski/Shutterstock.com; p. 6 pics721/Shutterstock.com;p. 7 Kelly vanDellen/Shutterstock.com; p. 9 quiggyt4/Shutterstock.com; p. 10 https://en.m.wikipedia.org/wiki/File:Flag_of_the_United_States_Department_of_the_Interior.svg; p. 11 https://en.m.wikipedia.org/wiki/File:Last_Danish_Parade_at_Saint_Croix.jpg; p. 13 railway fx/Shutterstock.com; p. 14 Todor Stoyanov/Shutterstock.com; p. 16 Limbitech/Shutterstock.com; p. 17 https://commons.wikimedia.org/wiki/File:Virgin_Islands_National_Guard_(36523271394).jpg; p. 18 Zoran Atanasoski/Shutterstock.com; p. 19 BlueBarronPhoto/Shutterstock.com; p. 20 Norm Diver/Shutterstock.com; p. 21 pics721/Shutterstock.com; p. 22 Nancy Pauwels/Shutterstock.com; p. 23 Dennis MacDonald/Shutterstock.com;p. 24 Debbie Ann Powell/Shutterstock.com; p. 25 EA Given/Shutterstock.com; p. 27 https://commons.wikimedia.org/wiki/File:Virgin_Islands_National_Guard_(36978307720).jpg; p. 28 https://commons.wikimedia.org/wiki/File:John_Trumbull_-_Alexander_Hamilton_-_Google_Art_Project_(499056).jpg.

Library of Congress Cataloging-in-Publication Data

Names: McDonnell, Julia, 1979- author.
Title: U.S. Virgin Islands / Julia McDonnell.
Description: New York : PowerKids Press, [2025] | Series: Territories of the United States | Includes index.
Identifiers: LCCN 2024004148 (print) | LCCN 2024004149 (ebook) | ISBN 9781725329195 (library binding) | ISBN 9781725329171 (paperback) | ISBN 9781725329201 (ebook)
Subjects: LCSH: United States Virgin Islands--Juvenile literature.
Classification: LCC F2136 .M33 2025 (print) | LCC F2136 (ebook) | DDC 972.97/22--dc23/eng/20240126
LC record available at https://lccn.loc.gov/2024004148
LC ebook record available at https://lccn.loc.gov/2024004149

Manufactured in the United States of America

Some of the images in this book illustrate individuals who are models. The depictions do not imply actual situations or events.

CPSIA Compliance Information: Batch #CSPK25. For further information contact Rosen Publishing at 1-800-237-9932.

CONTENTS

Welcome to the U.S. Virgin Islands

Did you know the United States has territories in addition to its 50 states? Some U.S. territories, such as the Northern Mariana Islands, are far from the mainland United States, but the territory called the U.S. Virgin Islands is a short plane ride away.

The U.S. Virgin Islands is in the northeastern Caribbean Sea and has a population of about 87,000 people, according to the 2020 U.S. **census**. It has three main islands and about 50 islets, or small islands, and cays, which are low islands of sand or coral. Saint Croix (KROY) is the largest island at 84 square miles (218 sq km). It has a population of about 41,000. Saint Thomas is smaller but has a slightly larger population. The third island, Saint John, is the smallest and has just a few thousand people.

FLAG OF THE U.S. VIRGIN ISLANDS

The capital of the U.S. Virgin Islands, Charlotte Amalie, is on Saint Thomas.

The Arrival of Outsiders

The Taíno, a people from northern South America, settled in the Virgin Islands about 3,000 years ago. They were farmers and fishers who built villages on the bays. Warlike Carib peoples arrived on the islands in the mid-1400s. The Caribs were the most powerful **culture** when the Spanish first made contact with the islands in 1493.

Europeans, including the Spanish, British, French, Dutch, and Danes, soon began competing for Caribbean land and resources. The Danish West India Company, which oversaw trade in the Caribbean for Denmark, built a colony on Saint Thomas in 1672.

The company expanded to Saint John in 1718 and Saint Croix in 1733. Plantations that grew **sugarcane**, cotton, and other crops made Europeans wealthy. Europeans enslaved **Indigenous** peoples. Thousands of Indigenous people died because of forced labor and European diseases.

AHOY, PIRATES!

By the 1600s, the Virgin Islands were full of European pirates. They plundered each other's ships and settlements, and the many islands served as places to escape or lurk. But pirates didn't always have to hide. Some had permanent bases, encouraged by the colonies because they participated in trade and caused trouble for other countries. Famous pirates who visited the Virgin Islands included Captain William Kidd, Stede Bonnet, and Black Sam Bellamy.

The Taíno left behind carvings called petroglyphs. Some petroglyphs found on Reef Bay Trail on the island of Saint John are more than 1,000 years old.

Islands of Enslavement

Slave trading became another source of wealth in the Danish West Indies, as Denmark's colony was called. Danish traders transported as many as 100,000 enslaved Africans to Saint Croix and sold them in slave markets. Saint John and Saint Croix relied on the plantation system. Saint Thomas had more trading and business opportunities because of its natural harbor.

Several uprisings challenged the enslavement system, including one in 1733 in which a group of enslaved people took over Saint John for six months. Eventually, a revolt on Saint Croix in July 1848 led to the end of slavery in the colony. Without forced labor, the plantation system weakened and profits too. Many workers, though now paid, weren't treated well, and some led **riots** in protest. The islands fell on hard times.

Territorial Truths ☆☆☆☆☆

In 1878, Mary Thomas (about 1848–1905) helped lead a protest of the unfair treatment of workers. The protestors burned buildings on more than 50 plantations and most of the town of Frederiksted on Saint Croix.

DIFFICULT LIVES

The enslaved people of the Virgin Islands lived hard lives, no matter what work they did. Those in the field toiled outside doing exhausting work. Craftsmen learned trades but could sometimes earn their own money. Those in the house, often women, had tasks such as laundry, cooking, cleaning, and childcare. Supervisors called bombas oversaw other enslaved workers and whole plantations. Enslaved people worked so hard that there were more deaths than births. Some managed to escape and live in the dense forests.

The ruins of the Annaberg Sugar Plantation on Saint John are a reminder of the industry that sustained the Virgin Islands for so many years—and the terrible treatment enslaved people endured.

From Colony to Territory

During World War I (1914–1918), the United States wanted territory in the Caribbean. The Danish West Indies had deep ports that could hold warships. It was also a key stop on the Panama Canal shipping route. In addition, Americans feared Germany could seize islands from which to launch strikes against the United States. In 1917, Denmark agreed to sell its territory to the United States for $25 million. The islands became known as the U.S. Virgin Islands.

After the war, the U.S. Navy managed the U.S. Virgin Islands, or USVI. Some conditions in the islands, which had been made worse by natural disasters, improved. The residents received U.S. citizenship in 1927. In 1931, the **U.S. Department of the Interior** took control. Still, residents were unhappy with appointed, rather than elected, officials.

U.S. DEPARTMENT OF THE INTERIOR SEAL

GETTING A VOICE

Citizenship was expanded in 1932 to any USVI natives, no matter where they lived. But power was still held by a governor appointed by the U.S. president. The Organic Act of the Virgin Islands, passed in 1936, set up limited self-government, with two councils. The Revised Organic Act went further in 1954, establishing three branches of government, including one main legislative, or lawmaking, body. Finally, in 1970, the first elections for a governor and lieutenant governor were held.

In this photo, the flag of Denmark is lowered for the last time, on March 31, 1917. That day, in which the United States took control of the Danish West Indies, is called Transfer Day.

An Unincorporated Territory

A Virgin Islander's citizenship isn't the same as the citizenship of someone born in the mainland United States. The USVI is an unincorporated territory. That means not all parts of the U.S. Constitution apply to its citizens.

For example, Virgin Islanders can't vote in U.S. presidential elections. That means they don't have any say in who becomes president—even though the president's decisions can have a big impact on life in the USVI.

Virgin Islanders can elect a representative to the U.S. Congress. But that person is a nonvoting member of the House of Representatives. Though they can serve on and vote in congressional committees, they can't vote as part of the whole House to pass a bill into law. They can, however, speak to the Congress about the USVI's needs.

Territorial Truths ☆☆☆☆☆

As U.S. citizens, Virgin Islanders receive U.S. military protection, aid after natural disasters, enrollment in federal programs, and the ability to travel or move to the United States at any time.

WHY DOES THE U.S. WANT TERRITORIES?

Having control over land and offshore areas has advantages for the United States when it comes to military and defense. It also expands the U.S. market for trading goods without tariffs, and the ports make shipping easier. The United States also gets access to natural resources and products. The top exports of the USVI are refined petroleum (oil), rum, clothing, boats, and watches. The USVI's total exports are worth more than $2 billion each year.

The flag the USVI uses today was authorized in 1921. The bald eagle—the national bird of the United States—represents the USVI's connection to the mainland. The three arrows it holds represent the three main islands.

On the Map

The U.S. Virgin Islands is part of the Virgin Islands archipelago. This archipelago, or large group of islands, is made up of about 90 islands of various sizes that stretch about 60 miles (97 km). The USVI is in the west of the archipelago. The British Virgin Islands, four large islands and 32 smaller islands, is in the east.

Many of these islands arose millions of years ago because of the movements of the giant pieces of rock, called tectonic plates, that make up Earth's outer layer. The USVI is located where the North American Plate meets the Caribbean Plate. Scientists think the plates' movements sparked underwater volcanoes. By about 22 million years ago, a lava mountain built up, creating Saint Thomas. Saint Croix and Saint John are likely the result of lava, ash, and coral reef deposits.

Territorial Truths

In 1996, the U.S. Department of the Interior returned Water Island, found in Charlotte Amalie Harbor of Saint Thomas, to the USVI. It became the fourth major island in the territory, with a population of about 160.

Some people place the U.S. Virgin Islands in the larger chain of islands called the Lesser Antilles. Others group these islands with those of the Greater Antilles chain.

How's the Weather?

On average, more than 2 million tourists visit the USVI every year to experience its natural beauty. They also come for the pleasant weather and warm ocean waters.

The climate is tropical, which means it's warm and sunny year round with humid, or moist, air. The average winter air temperature is 77°F (25°C), and summer's average air temperature is slightly higher at 82°F (28°C). The average water temperature stays between 79° and 83°F (26° and 28°C).

While the USVI doesn't have a rainy season, some months experience rain more than others. Some of the wettest months are August through November. But even during these times, rain showers tend to be short. Hurricane season is from June to September. These powerful storms mostly take place in August and September.

HURRICANE IRMA

Territorial Truths ☆☆☆☆☆

Tradewinds that travel across the Atlantic carry tons (literally!) of dust from Africa to the Caribbean. That dust brings pollutants, fungi, and bacteria to the USVI.

The USVI mostly experiences pleasant weather, but hurricanes are a danger. In 2017, two major hurricanes, Irma and Maria, hit the islands. They damaged more than 90 percent of the buildings.

Land and Sea

For years, European colonists cleared the Virgin Islands' forests for plantations. Today, about 60 percent of the lands are covered by forest. The trees tend to be young and in higher elevations. Shorter, woody plants called scrub are closer to shore.

A few plants in the USVI should be avoided. Their names reflect that, including stinging nettle, death apple, prickly pear, and deadly nightshade. The ginger thomas, a flowering shrub, though not native to the Americas, is the official flower of the USVI.

Birds, **rodents**, bats, and lizards are plentiful, including iguanas 6 feet (1.8 m) long and the bananaquit, the official bird of the islands. Europeans brought mongooses to control rats. Donkeys and goats were also introduced to the islands and freely wander today.

IGUANA

SURVIVING AND THRIVING

In a tropical spot, would you expect to see a "dry forest"? The name just means the trees live in a place that can experience months without much rain. They don't get as tall as mainland forests because the sea salt and wind patterns affect their growth. Some species, such as the wattapama and Tyre palm, grow well on the steep slopes of Saint Thomas and Saint Croix. Others, such as seagrape and frangipani, do better on the flatter landscape of Saint John.

The Turk's Cap cactus plant grows on Saint John and produces red flowers, which are a favorite snack of goats and birds. People report they taste like kiwi fruit.

The waters around USVI are full of life, including many species of fish, lobsters, sea turtles, urchins, hermit crabs, and conchs, a kind of sea snail. Dolphins and whales can be spotted at certain times of the year.

The coral reefs around the USVI support much of this **biodiversity**. Reefs are a living **habitat** made up of thousands of individual corals in a colony. Each polyp, a small tubelike creature, has a mouth, stomach, and arms. It makes a protective "skeleton" from the water's calcium, a chemical element. Coral species often get their names based on what they look like. Finger, lettuce leaf, brain, elkhorn, and pillar coral can all be found in the USVI. Reefs are a safe place for many marine animals to feed, rest, hide, and breed.

COKI REEF

YELLOWSTONE, EVERGLADES, ACADIA... AND THE VIRGIN ISLANDS?

You can find one of the 63 U.S. national parks in the USVI. About two-thirds of Saint John is occupied by the Virgin Islands National Park. More than 3,000 years of history are preserved, including sites and **artifacts** from the Taíno people through the time of Danish colonialism. And from hiking in the mountains and camping near the beach to snorkeling in the coral reefs and boating among the islands, there's something for just about every visitor to enjoy.

Hurricane Hole in Saint John, shown here, is the only coastal part of the Virgin Islands Coral Reef National Monument, which was established to protect the coral reefs and other habitats in the area.

Keeping the USVI Running

After the plantation system ended, the economy of the islands weakened, though sugarcane and cotton were still money-producing crops. Saint Thomas's harbor was also a favorite for traders and merchants, which added to the economy.

However, tourism is key in modern times. Virgin Islanders have jobs in hotels, restaurants, shops, and entertainment. Others work in agriculture, manufacturing, and construction. The government also provides employment.

The USVI's government is modeled after the federal and state systems. The executive branch is led by an elected governor and lieutenant governor. Fifteen elected senators form the legislative branch: seven each from Saint Thomas and Saint Croix and one from Saint John. The judicial branch has three levels of courts: district courts, superior courts, and the supreme court.

Territorial Truths ☆☆☆☆☆

The USVI once had a booming oil industry. The closing of a large **refinery** on Saint Croix in 2012 caused a financial crisis. The refinery restarted in 2021 but was shut down again due to air pollution.

The USVI has two airports, but many visitors arrive and depart by boat. In 2022, about 1.6 million people came to the islands, and over 777,000 of them were on cruise ships.

The People of the USVI

Because of colonialism and slavery, the population of the USVI today is mostly a mix of African, Danish, Dutch, British, Spanish, and French backgrounds. In the 2020 census, about 71 percent identified as Black or African American, and around 13 percent identified as white. One percent or less reported they were Asian, American Indian, or Native Hawaiian. Another 6 percent identified as "some other race," and 7.5 percent chose the label "two or more races."

More than 70 percent of Virgin Islanders speak English as their main language. About 17 percent report they speak Spanish or Spanish Creole, and another 8.5 percent speak French or French Creole. Creoles are languages that developed in the 1600s and 1700s between groups of people who couldn't communicate, especially European colonists and enslaved African and Indigenous peoples.

A 230-YEAR-OLD SAINT THOMAS CHURCH

Territorial Truths ☆☆☆☆☆

Europeans and Americans influenced USVI architecture, or building design, but Virgin Islanders put their own colorful mark on many of the structures on the islands.

Virgin Islanders celebrate their culture. Visitors can see traditional clothing, dance, music, and more during certain festivals.

A Paradise with Challenges

Tourism on the U.S. Virgin Islands suffered after the 2017 hurricanes and the 2020 COVID-19 **pandemic**. The USVI had relied on that income. **Inflation** made costs higher—and many things were already costly. But salaries for many people didn't keep up, and unemployment increased. These factors and others, such as fewer educational opportunities, caused people to leave the USVI. The population fell by 18 percent between 2010 and 2020.

These aren't the only trials facing the island. Its plant and animal life are at risk from overfishing, pollution, and overdevelopment. Disposal of trash and sewage is challenging, and landfills are almost full. Repairs and upgrades to roads, bridges, ports, and electrical lines are needed. Residents hope the wise use of federal funds and more businesses will improve life in the USVI.

Territorial Truths ☆☆☆☆☆

Because so many people visit the USVI's beaches, the concentration of sunscreen chemicals in its waters is high. This harms the living creatures of the coral reefs.

ONE THING THE USVI WANTS

The USVI relies on rain for most of its fresh water. Water can be purchased, but it can be costly. Most residents store rainwater that runs off their roofs in underground containers called cisterns. But rainfall is expected to decrease in the Caribbean by 2050, perhaps by 50 percent, according to the U.S. government report called the Fourth National Climate Assessment. Another method of getting fresh water, though time-consuming, is a technology called desalination, which takes salt out of salt water. Saint Thomas and Saint Croix have desalination plants.

The USVI has had its own National Guard since 1973. The members of this military force can help all around the world, but its specialty is disaster relief—often close to home.

Influential Islanders

Famous Virgin Islanders are familiar to many on the U.S. mainland. Founding Father Alexander Hamilton (1757–1804) spent his early years on Saint Croix, where he worked in Christiansted. Later, he served in the army under George Washington, helped write the U.S. Constitution, and became the first U.S. secretary of the treasury.

More recently, basketball legend Tim Duncan, born in 1976, grew up on Saint Croix with dreams of greatness—in swimming. In 1989, Hurricane Hugo destroyed the pool he trained in, so Duncan switched to basketball. He became an NBA (National Basketball Association) Most Valuable Player and All Star, among other honors.

The motto of the USVI—"United in Pride and Hope" —reflects that, despite challenges, Virgin Islanders have much **optimism** and love for their home.

ALEXANDER HAMILTON

TIMELINE

About 1500 BCE — People migrate from South America and settle in the islands.

1493 — Christopher Columbus sails to the islands on behalf of Spain.

1625 — The British and Dutch claim territory on Saint Croix.

1672 — The Danish West India Company builds a colony on Saint Thomas.

1718 — Saint John is settled by the Danish West India Company.

1733 — The Danish West India Company buys Saint Croix from France.

1848 — Slavery is abolished in the Danish West Indies.

1917 — The United States purchases the Danish territory for $25 million.

1927 — U.S. Virgin Islanders are given U.S. citizenship.

1936 — The Organic Act gives Virgin Islanders some self-government.

1954 — The revised Organic Act establishes three branches of government.

1970 — Elections for a USVI governor and lieutenant governor are held for the first time.

2017 — Hurricanes Irma and Maria strike within two weeks of each other, causing major damage.

Glossary

artifact: Something made by humans in the past.

biodiversity: The different kinds of life in an environment shown by numbers of different kinds of plants and animals.

census: The official process of counting the number of things and collecting information about them.

culture: The beliefs and ways of life of a group of people.

habitat: The natural home for plants, animals, and other living things.

indigenous: Having to do with the earliest known people of a place.

inflation: A continual increase in the price of goods and services.

optimism: Expecting good things to happen.

pandemic: A time or event in which a disease spreads quickly and affects a large number of people in a wide area or around the world.

refinery: A place that removes unwanted substances from a resource, producing a purer form of it.

riot: A public disturbance during which a group of people take action.

rodent: A small, furry animal with large front teeth, such as a mouse or rat.

sugarcane: A tall grass grown in warm places for sugar.

U.S. Department of the Interior: The part of the U.S. government that oversees federal lands.

For More Information

Books

Callender, Kacen. *Hurricane Child.* New York, NY: Scholastic Press, 2018.

Leed, Percy. *Tim Duncan: Power Forward.* Minneapolis, MN: Lerner Publications, 2022.

Tornio, Stacy. *The National Parks Scavenger Hunt: A Family-Friendly Way to Explore All 63 Parks.* Portland, OR: Timber Press, 2023.

Websites

Annaberg Sugar Plantation
www.cyark.org/projects/annaberg-sugar-plantation/overview
Learn about slavery and colonialism on this sugar plantation.

National Park Service: Virgin Islands
www.nps.gov/state/vi/index.htm
Explore the national monuments, historic sites, and preserves found in the USVI.

United States Virgin Islands: Facts and Stats
www.britannica.com/facts/United-States-Virgin-Islands
Review some key facts and check out photos and maps.

INDEX